The Edge

A play

Steve Carley

Samuel French
New York-Toronto-

THE EDGE

First presented in the McCarthy Auditorium at the Stephen Joseph Theatre, Scarborough, on 10th September 1997, with the following cast:

The Doctor	Colin Gourley
Marcus Adams	Richard Freeman
Stuart Wade	Nicholas Haverson

Directed by Connal Orton
Designed by Pip Leckenby
Lighting by Paul Towson
Music by John Pattison

CHARACTERS

Marcus Adams: *a successful stockbroker; approaching 50*
The Doctor: *Marcus's psychiatrist**
Stuart Wade: *Marcus's junior partner*

The action takes place in two London offices; that of Marcus Adams and that of his Doctor

Time — the present, and the past, and the future

NOTE

* Although **The Doctor** is referred to throughout the script as being male (and being called Paul) it is perfectly acceptable for a woman to perform this role, with an appropriate change of name.

With grateful thanks to
Stefan Gleisner
for his advice, encouragement and constructive abuse

THE EDGE

A stockbroker's office and a psychiatrist's office

The set is in two areas. One is the stockbroker's office of Marcus Adams and Stuart Wade and has two desks, each with a chair, a telephone and computer terminal and the usual office equipment; there is also a stationery cupboard. A practical light-fitting is situated overhead. The other area, a psychiatrist's office, can take the simpler form of a desk and two chairs

The Lights come up on the psychiatrist's office. The Doctor is sitting at his desk, reading a case file. After a few moments he looks at his watch, goes to his door and opens it

Doctor Would you like to come in?

Marcus Adams enters. He is fifty and wears an expensive, but crumpled, suit. He looks slightly haggard and highly agitated

Marcus About time.
Doctor (*closing the door and sitting*) Sit down.

Marcus sits in the chair opposite the Doctor and immediately lights a cigarette

You look tired.
Marcus I — haven't slept.
Doctor How are you feeling?
Marcus How the bloody hell do you *think* I feel? I'm out of time!
Doctor No change, then?
Marcus No.
Doctor It is still at five o'clock?

Marcus (*impatiently*) Yes! (*He takes a long drag on his cigarette*) Paul, what am I going to do?

The Doctor scribbles something in his notepad, sets it down, then leans back in his chair

Doctor Firstly, I want you to tell me exactly what happened.

Marcus I've already told you.

Doctor I know certain aspects from our last session. And your phone call yesterday was slightly — slightly confusing. For me to be of any help, I need a much more comprehensive picture than I have at the moment.

Marcus There isn't time for that!

Doctor Marcus ——

Marcus (*standing*) This is *it,* Paul! I'm out of time! It'll be here at five o'clock! I haven't got time to chat!

Doctor We have to talk this through, Marcus, or there's no point in having this session.

A pause

Marcus Exactly what do you need to know?

Doctor Everything.

Marcus Paul, there isn't time!

Doctor We have an hour.

Marcus You might have an hour! I've got — (*he looks at his watch*) I've got forty minutes!

Doctor It's up to you. We can just sit and wait until five o'clock, or we can try to do something about it.

A pause

Marcus (*sitting*) All right. Just hurry up.

Doctor Good. Now. In your own time.

Marcus (*putting his cigarette out and immediately lighting another*) Well — after I saw you last week things began to change …

Doctor From the beginning, Marcus.

A pause. Marcus looks at his watch

It's necessary.

Marcus From the beginning ... (*He takes a long drag of his cigarette*) Well... I first started to suspect something was different about two weeks ago as you know.

Doctor What was your initial reaction?

Marcus I didn't realize what was happening at first. Well, who would? They were just little things. Things that happen every day. Things that people laugh about, but pay no attention to. Odd — coincidences. The sort that always happen to people ... But, thinking about it, it started before then. Not the coincidences, just — something — a feeling. Mind you, the coincidences *could* have been happening before that and I just didn't notice. No, I first noticed when I was late for work. Twenty minutes late! That really threw me. I'm never late. Never. I just slept in for some reason. And when I woke up I felt *different* somehow, out of sorts — out of *synch*. Yes, out of synch.

The Lights cross-fade from the psychiatrist's office to the stockbroker's office during the following line

At the time I just put it down to the panic of being late. But it wasn't that. It was something else ...

The phone in the stockbroker's office rings

Stuart Wade enters with a cup of coffee which he puts on his desk. He answers the phone

Marcus leaves the psychiatrist's office during the following

Stuart (*into the phone*) "Adams and Wade". Stuart speaking. ... No, I'm afraid Mr Adams has — (*he glances at his watch*) — has stepped out of the office for a moment. This is Stuart Wade, his partner. Can I help? ... Right. ... Yes, that is more Mr Adams's field. ... Can I get him to call you back? ... Right, hang on. ... (*He*

finds a message pad and pen) Yes. Go on. … Is that with one "t"
or two?... Right. … And what is it concerning? ... I see, yes. …
And what's your number?… Right. … OK, Mr Whitaker, I'll see
that he returns your call as soon as he gets back. … Yes. … Right,
thank you, Mr Whitaker. … Goodbye. (*He hangs up and starts to
write the message out fully*)

*Marcus rushes in, breathing hard. As in all his "recalled" scenes,
Marcus has a noticeable change in his attire, and has no sign of
the strain he shows in his "present-day" scenes*

Marcus Oh, God. I'm sorry, Stuart.
Stuart Traffic?
Marcus No, no. I just — slept in.
Stuart Slept in? You? You're not ill, are you? It's getting chaotic
enough around here without you ...

*Marcus hangs his coat up, sits at his desk and switches on his
computer*

Marcus No, no, I feel fine. A bit — "fazed", maybe. I don't think
I've woken up properly. What did Whitaker want?
Stuart He wants to talk to you about ... (*A pause*) How did you know
he'd rung?
Marcus (*not concentrating*) Who, Whitaker?
Stuart Yeah.
Marcus Didn't you tell me?
Stuart No.
Marcus Oh — well, I must have heard you talking to him. What
did he want?
Stuart He wants to talk to you about an option.
Marcus On what?
Stuart It's a new company. They're in computer-aided design.
They're called ——
Marcus⎫
Stuart ⎬ (*together*) — Microtech.
Stuart (*giving Marcus a look*) Yeah … How did you know?

Marcus Lucky guess.
Stuart Oh … (*He works for a moment*) Who is he, anyway?
Marcus Who?
Stuart Whitaker.
Marcus No idea.
Stuart (*confused*) Oh.
Marcus What?
Stuart Nothing. I just thought you said that … Well, it sounded like you knew him.
Marcus I don't think I do … Maybe someone… (*He suddenly glances at his phone*)
Stuart What's wrong?

The phone rings. Marcus picks the phone up and speaks immediately, without waiting to see who the caller is

Marcus (*into the phone*) Hi, Clare. … No, don't worry, I'm fine now. … I don't know what it was, I just felt a bit strange. … (*He looks at his watch*) Er, about twenty minutes. What about you?… Oh God, I'm sorry, just blame me. … Oh, you did, *fine*. … Look, I've got to go. I missed an important call and he's ringing back in a minute. … OK, I'll see you then. … Bye. (*He hangs up*)
Stuart Who's ringing back?
Marcus Whitaker.
Stuart No, he's not.

Stuart hands Marcus the message he had written previously

He wanted *you* to ring *him* as soon as you got in. (*He returns to his desk*)
Marcus Are you sure?
Stuart That's what he said.
Marcus Oh — right then, let's see what Microtech turns up … (*He starts keying into his computer*)

Stuart gets back to his work. After a few moments …

Marcus ⎫
Stuart ⎬ (*together*) Fancy a drink at lunchtime?

They look at each other

   (*Together*) The *Nelson*?

They smile

Stuart Great minds think alike…
Marcus ⎫
Stuart ⎬ (*together*) Fools seldom differ.
Stuart (*chuckling*) Spooky.

They settle into their work. After a few seconds Marcus glances up at the overhead light and sighs

   Now what's wrong?

Marcus goes to the stationery cupboard and begins to search through it

   What are you looking for?
Marcus (*emerging from the cupboard holding a light bulb*) There. I knew we had one.
Stuart What's that for?

There is a popping sound and the stage is suddenly plunged into darkness. A pause

   I don't believe it — Marcus, how the hell did you —— ?

The phone rings

   Oh, Christ — now what?
Marcus It's Whitaker. (*During the following he climbs on to a chair and changes the old light bulb for the new one*)

Stuart, cursing and fumbling, finds the phone in the dark. He finally answers it

Stuart (*into the phone*) Hallo? Oh, *hallo,* Mr Whitaker. ... Er, no. ... No, I'm sorry, Mr Adams is, er... He hasn't returned yet. ... Yes. ... Oh, I see. ... And you're leaving now, are you?... Right, well, have you got a mobile?... Good, hang on. (*He searches for pen and paper and finds them*) Go on. ... Yes. ... Right, I've got it. ... I'll get him to ring you as soon as he returns. ... Yes. ... Goodbye. (*He hangs up*) Marcus?

Marcus Yeah?

Stuart Marcus, will you please tell me how the hell you knew the light was going to blow?

Marcus I didn't. Well, I don't — I don't think I did. I was just wondering if we had a spare. It was just a coincidence.

Stuart "A coincidence"? What about Whitaker ringing back? Another coincidence, I suppose.

The Lights snap back on. Marcus is revealed standing on the chair, having just replaced the old light bulb. He puts the chair back, sits at his desk and starts working

Well?

Marcus What?

Stuart Care to offer an explanation?

Marcus For what?

Stuart For what? For — for these spooky coincidences of yours! Is this a wind-up, or have you turned into Mystic Meg?

Marcus What are you talking about?

Stuart From the moment you walked in you've been ——

Marcus What time is it?

Stuart What?

Marcus The time.

Stuart (*looking at his watch*) Oh God, I've got to go. I said I'd meet Fisher ten minutes ago. I'll see you in the *Nelson*, all right? (*He puts some papers into his briefcase and goes to the door*) And if I bump into Mulder and Scully on the way down, I'll tell them you're expecting them.

Marcus Very funny.
Stuart See you.
Marcus Bye.

Stuart exits

Marcus immediately stops working and sits in thought for a few moments, looking up at the light overhead with concern. He then returns to his work. Suddenly, he looks at his phone. After a second it rings. He moves his hand to pick it up, then snatches it back. The phone continues to ring. Eventually he answers it

> (*Into the phone*) Hallo?… Yes, speaking. … (*There is a long silence as he listens to the call*) Yes, I'm still here. … Thank you for letting me know. (*He hangs up*)

The Lights go down to two tight spots, one on Marcus and one on the Doctor. They both look straight out towards the audience

Doctor That must have been difficult for you. How did he die? You didn't tell me.
Marcus In his sleep. He'd — er — he'd been ill for some time. Lung cancer …
Doctor I'm sorry. Were you close to your father?
Marcus Yes.

A pause

> But that's not why I'm telling you about it. The point is that I *knew*. I *knew* my father had died *before I* picked the phone up — I *felt* it. I *felt* that he was dead! I mean, I was upset about it. I still am very upset about it. But I'm not here because my father *died*. I'm here because I *knew* my father had died. Don't you see? It was another "spooky coincidence"! But it *wasn't* a coincidence. I was *sensing* things that were about to happen. Obviously, I thought it was all just my imagination. That I was just tired. But it just kept happening. More and more frequently. Eventually it was like I

was living a second ahead of everything else. It was disrupting everything. I couldn't sleep. I couldn't eat. I couldn't even tell anyone because they'd think I was cracking up. But I had to tell someone. That's when I came to see you.

The Light fades on the Doctor during the following; once the Blackout is complete, he makes a small adjustment to his appearance to signify a shift in time

I told you all about it, but I could tell that you didn't believe a word I was saying. But I proved it to you, didn't I? You were saying it was all my imagination, just intuition, and that it was all because of my fears of the future. At one point, you were going on about a girl in a red coat, for some reason ——

The Light on Marcus slowly fades. A single light comes back up on the Doctor. Marcus returns to his seat in the psychiatrist's office and alters his clothing back to its original state

Doctor We can communicate clearly with others, and with ourselves, by using words. But we can know things without using words. For instance, we know that the girl is wearing a red coat because we see that the coat is red. Intuition is based on more subtle sense impressions which we cannot describe in words. We know that the girl has a red coat in her wardrobe because we "can tell" that she is "the kind of girl who likes red coats". Intuition is the acquiring of knowledge through sensory contact with the object, without the "intuitor" being able to explain exactly how he came to these conclusions. In other words, intuition means that we can know something without knowing *how* we know it.

The Lights come up fully on the psychiatrist's office

It is subconscious knowledge without words, based on subconscious observations without words, and in the right circumstances it can be more reliable and accurate than conscious knowledge based on conscious observation. What appears to be clairvoyance or mental telepathy, however, is based on something else. Something else that makes us suddenly suspect, for no known reason, that the girl's older sister has *two* red coats.

During the following, Marcus mouths the Doctor's words as he is speaking them

There is evidence, however, that perceived mental telepathy may be a function of the deeper layers of the mind. Such occurrences have been documented by leading psychologists, but there is no way of proving the veracity of these events. I've never come across it, nor am I likely to.

Marcus audibly joins in

Marcus ⎫
Doctor ⎭ (*together*) In your case, however, I would suggest that
                           most of ——

The Doctor looks at Marcus

Doctor I'm sorry, Marcus, did you want to say something?
Marcus No, carry on…

A pause. Again Marcus joins in with the Doctor's words. They speak simultaneously, and with equal strength

Marcus ⎫
Doctor ⎭ (*together*) In your case, however, I would suggest that
                           most of ——

Again, the Doctor looks at Marcus. Marcus mirrors the Doctor's movements precisely during the following

—— most of what —— most of what you are experiencing is —— coincidence —— and the rest —— the rest —— is pure imagination. Marcus this is —— this is fantastic! It can't be true! How do you know what I'm going to say? Marcus!

They stand simultaneously

Marcus!

They point at each other

You — you know what I am going to do! This is absolutely — incredible! It's true! Everything you said — was true!

A pause. They move their heads slowly toward each other over the desk until they are nose to nose. Another pause

PENGUIN!

Black-out

Stuart enters and sits at his desk

Stuart's phone rings. The Lights come back up on the stockbroker's office, where Stuart is working at his desk. He answers the phone

Stuart (*into the phone*) "Adams and Wade". ... Oh, hallo, Mr Whitaker. ... How's Microtech working out?... That's great. ... Yes, he is. ... Yes. ... I don't know how he does it, he seems to have the edge at the moment. ... Yes. ... I'm sorry, he isn't in the office today. A funeral. ... Yes, it is. ... Can I help?... Yes. ... What sort of flutter?... Yes, well it's always best to double-check when you're dealing with the housing market. ... Who did he suggest?... *Marshall's?*... *The house-builders.* ... Are you sure?... I thought they were about to go under, their shares are more or less worthless. ... All right, please hold on a moment, Mr Whitaker, and I'll check it out. (*He puts Whitaker on "hold" and tries to find information on the computer*)

The Lights come up on the psychiatrist's office

Doctor Ah yes, the funeral. When was that?

Marcus About five or six days later. By now I had realized that I
was developing the gift of foresight. And it *was* developing —
almost proportionally. It seemed that for every day that passed I
could see another day further into the future. It was incredible.

Doctor What was Stuart's reaction to all this?

Marcus I didn't tell him. He's always saying that to be successful
you need to be one step ahead of everyone else. You need an edge.
Well, what better edge for a broker to have than to be able to see
into the future? But it doesn't work like that. If I *had* told him and
he believed me, which I doubt, he'd have thought we could make
millions from it. That's all he thinks about. But that sort of thing
doesn't interest me any more. I've made more than enough
money to keep Clare and I comfortable for the rest of our lives.

Doctor Did you tell Clare?

Marcus I tried to, but she didn't understand. She thought I was
talking about our *plans* for the future.

Doctor Plans?

Marcus We more or less agreed that on my fiftieth birthday I'd sell
my half of the business to Stuart and retire.

Doctor And how did you feel about that?

Marcus Well — I — I had mixed feelings about it.

A pause

(*Suddenly looking at his watch and leaping to his feet*) Christ!
There's only twenty minutes left! (*He paces, anxiously*) Are you
sure those tests showed nothing? They couldn't have made a
mistake?

Doctor No.

Marcus (*angrily*) Well, what the hell is it, then?

Doctor I don't know, Marcus. In the meantime let's carry on, shall
we?

A pause

Shall we?

A pause

Marcus (*sitting*) All right, all right. Where had I got to?

Doctor You could see almost a week into the future.

Marcus Yes. You'd think that would be a gift, wouldn't you? Well, it would have been if I could have controlled it. Like I said, it doesn't work like that. It's not as if I could conjure up next week's winning lottery numbers, or anything. They were just random flashes, and they always related to me, or what was going on around me. Like with you. I didn't consciously try to predict what you were going to say, it just came to me. (*He smiles*) Penguin... (*He bursts out laughing*) Your face. I thought you were going to pass out!

Doctor Yes ... it was — it was a very memorable incident.

Marcus I bet you thought you were going mad.

Doctor Yes... (*He refers to his notepad*) So, Marcus, it was five or six days later. You could see almost a week into the future, but your premonitions were not as frequent or as clear as they were. And you'd just been to your father's funeral ...

The Light fades out on the psychiatrist's office

Marcus exits and changes into a mourning suit during the following

Stuart takes Whitaker off "hold"

Stuart (*into the phone*) Mr Whitaker, are you still there?... Right, well I've been through every source I can think of, and I can't find any news about Marshall's whatsoever. ... Yes. ... And I was right about their shares, they're trading at one sixty-fourth of a penny apiece. Look, exactly what did Marcus say?... Bought out?... By whom?... You're kidding. ... No, I think shocked is more the word. ... No, no, I'd go for it if I were you. Marcus's intuition seems to be on the money at the moment. ... Yes. ... OK, how much should I put you down for?... Right. ... OK, consider it done. ... All right, goodbye. (*He hangs up and thinks for a couple of moments, then writes something down and slips the piece of paper into his pocket*)

Marcus enters

Hi. How did it go?

Marcus (*sitting at his desk*) Not too bad. There weren't too many people there, unfortunately. Most of Dad's generation are gone now, so Clare and I and a few people from the Home were the only ones there. Jo and Amanda are still in Hong Kong, and couldn't get the time off. They were both very upset. They were very close to their grandfather.

Stuart Oh, I'm sorry, Marcus.

Marcus No, it's fine, honestly. I knew who would be there, so it wasn't a surprise.

Stuart That's not too bad then.

A pause

Marcus Stu... I need to talk to you.

Stuart (*lighting a cigarette*) Sounds ominous. What about?

Marcus The future.

Stuart The future?

Marcus Well, more specifically, our future.

Stuart Go on.

Marcus I'm giving it up, Stu. I want you to buy me out.

Stuart What?

Marcus I've — I've had enough. I've lived and breathed the Market for thirty years, and I need to stop. I ——

Stuart You just need a rest. A holiday would sort you out.

Marcus No, Stu, I'm sorry. Clare and I have been talking about it for over a year now. It's wearing me down. I've been getting anxiety attacks, and I haven't been able to sleep for weeks now ...

Stuart You've been under a lot of strain, with your father and everything.

Marcus Look, I don't really want to get into it right now. I just thought you should know.

Stuart Marcus, you just said that you lived and breathed the business. Well, if that's true, then you can't just stop. You love this game. It makes you who you are. Besides, what are you going

to do? Play golf? Watch TV? A spot of gardening? That's not you.
Remember Henderson? He retired five years ago and he was your
age. Look what happened to him — they buried him last year!

Marcus Yes, I know all that. But it's what we've decided. It's not
fair to Clare. I spend all my waking hours away from home. We
never get to see each other. Stu, I missed my kids growing up.

A pause

Stuart Look, I've got a meeting in half an hour and I've got to get
up to speed on it. You go home and we'll talk about this tomorrow.
I've got the morning clear.

Marcus (*going to the door*) OK. I'm — I'm sorry…

Stuart We'll talk tomorrow.

Marcus exits

The phone rings. Stuart answers it

(*Into the phone*) "Adams and Wade".

Marcus enters

Stuart spea ——

Marcus Stu.

Stuart (*into the phone*) I'm sorry, please hold. (*He puts his hand
over the mouthpiece. To Marcus*) Yeah?

Marcus One more thing. Tell Clare I *hate* surprise birthdays.

Marcus exits

A pause

Stuart (*into the phone*) "Adams and Wade". Stuart speaking (*He
glances at the door*) Clare, hi. … How did it go?… Yes, Marcus
was saying, it's a shame. … No, he's just left. … The what?…

Funny you should mention that. I think we'd better call it off. We've been rumbled ...

The Lights go down on the stockbroker's office and a single light comes up on the Doctor

Marcus enters and takes his place at the Doctor's desk

Doctor Marcus, there were a lot of events occurring in your life which incorporate some sense of loss. Firstly, and perhaps most traumatically, there was the loss of your father. And with that comes the realization that you are now the sole representative of the oldest generation of your family. That is a milestone event in any person's life — the end of one chapter and the start of another. We also have the end of your career. You have spent your entire adult life striving to achieve your ambition of success in the Stock Market. You have achieved it. Success has been your driving force. You achieved career success. You achieved financial success. You achieved a successful marriage. You have successful children. And with this success you have lost the focus of your driving force. You have nothing left to achieve. It is also becoming clear that your age is another contributory factor.

The Lights come up on the rest of the psychiatrist's office, revealing Marcus in his chair opposite the Doctor

The fact that you wished to avoid celebrating your fiftieth birthday suggests that you may be experiencing a sense of your own mortality, which ——

Marcus Paul, I've got ten minutes left and all you can do is spout shit! It's coming, Paul. It's coming bloody fast and I don't know what to do! I feel so — so bloody helpless ... (*He stares into space*)

Doctor Yes, I know and I'm sorry. But we must carry on. Now, I just want to clarify the events of last week. At that point you could see a week into the future. Was it then that your gift stopped growing?

A pause

Is that right, Marcus?

Marcus Sorry?

Doctor Was it last week that your — premonitions stopped developing?

Marcus Yes. It just stayed where it was. The next day I could still only see a week into the future. I thought I'd have to spend the rest of my life like that. Being able to see a week into the future. Can you imagine it?

Doctor But it didn't stay like that.

Marcus No. The next day I could only see forward six days — a day less. The next day it was only five days … (*Impatiently*) You know all this! I rang and told you!

Doctor Yes, I remember. I'm just clarifying the issue. So, your gift hadn't merely reached its peak, it was starting to regress?

Marcus (*snapping*) Yes! (*After a pause; calming down*) It seemed to be regressing at exactly the same rate as it had grown — I was losing one day per day, if you see what I mean. "Great," I thought, "it was just temporary. By this time next week I'll be back to normal. I can get on with my life… my *new* life", whatever *that* was going to be now.

Doctor Had you made any plans?

Marcus Not really. Just that Clare and I decided to go on a long holiday as a combined celebration of my retirement and my "half-century". A skiing holiday. Actually, it was when we were talking about it yesterday that it hit me.

Doctor That something was wrong.

Marcus Yes.

Doctor And this was yesterday?

Marcus (*patiently*) Yes, just before I phoned you. I'd come in to go over some of the sign-over details with Stu. He was on the phone when I got there …

The Lights go down on the psychiatrist's office, and come up on the stockbroker's office. Stuart is at his desk, talking on the phone

Stuart (*into the phone*) That's great. It's just what you both need.
... Yes.... Are you looking forward to it?... Great. And have you
decided where you're going yet?... Skiing? Where?... St Moritz?
Fantastic! ... Yes, I know you have. We went there on our
honeymoon. I don't think I've ever enjoyed myself so much in my
whole life. Didn't do much skiing, though. ... (*He laughs*) When
are you going?... Tomorrow? Wow! I'm really jealous, Clare.
You'll have a wonderful time. ... Oh, he'll be all right. I think he's
just been a bit stressed out with everything. ... Yes. ... Good
news, what good news? ... Oh yes, the investment. Well, it was a
small house-building operation that was about to collapse ——

Marcus enters and takes his coat off

(*Waving to Marcus*) —— and I had some *inside information* that it
was about to be taken over. ... Yes, I did very nicely in the end.
... Yeah, thanks. ... Listen, Marcus has just arrived. I'll put him
on. ... Yes, you too. ... Talk to you soon. ... Bye... (*To Marcus*)
Clare.

Marcus (*going to his desk*) Oh, cheers.

Stuart And happy birthday.

Marcus There's nothing happy about it. (*He picks up his phone,
presses a button and sits down*)

Stuart hangs up

Hi, Clare, are you all packed?... I thought you would be. ... No,
I'm fine, a lot better now. ... Yes. ... More what?... Cards?... No,
you open them and put them on my desk. I'll look at them when
I get back. ... Well, it may be an important day for some people,
but not for me. I'd really prefer to forget about it. ... Yes. ... Just
treat it like any other day. ... All right then, we can go out for a
meal tonight if you want. ... No, of course I don't mind. ...
Tomorrow?... Well, I'm going to be busy winding things up here
for most of the day, and the lawyer is due at —— (*He looks
enquiringly at Stuart*)

Stuart Half-four.

Marcus — half-four for the sign-over, so I should be finished by five. ... Yes, it is a bit late, but we'll have plenty of time to make the flight ... Yes, five, I promise. I have nothing after that. ... No, that's *it, nothing, the end.* ... (*He laughs*) No, you can't have it in writing. ... On my honour, Clare, there's nothing, *absolutely nothing* after... after... (*Realization; to himself*) Five o'clock ... (*He slowly lays the receiver on the desk and rises;softly*) Shit.

Stuart (*looking up*) What's wrong?

Marcus (*not hearing*) Five o'clock...

Stuart What about it?

Marcus (*panic setting in*) Shit!

Stuart (*going over to Marcus*) Marcus, what the hell's wrong?

Marcus That's why— oh my God...

Stuart Marcus — Marcus, Clare's still on the phone ...

Marcus Oh my God!

Stuart (*shouting*) Marcus!

Marcus looks at Stuart

(*Pointing at the phone; quietly*) Clare.

Marcus looks at the phone, then picks it up

Marcus (*into the phone*) Sorry, Clare. I — I just — realized something. I have to go. (*He hangs up*)

Stuart Marcus, what's wrong?

Marcus Oh my God — five o'clock!

Stuart You're not making sense.

Marcus Five o'clock!

Stuart What about it?

Marcus I can't see past five o'clock! (*He paces up and down*)

Stuart Marcus ...

Marcus Christ, this is a nightmare! This is absolutely insane!

Stuart Marcus, will you please tell me what the bloody hell is going on!

Marcus searches his desk-top

What are you looking for?

Marcus finds a phone number and dials it

Are you going to tell me what's wrong, or not?

Marcus I'm sorry, Stu. I can't. It's — it's personal. ... (*Into the phone*) Hallo? I need to speak to Paul urgently. ... I don't *care* if he's with someone, I need to speak to him! *Now!* ... *Yes,* it's an emergency! ... Marcus Adams. ... *Thank you.* ...

Stuart Is there anything I can do?

Marcus No... (*He pauses*) Yes — yes, there is.

Stuart What?

Marcus Give me a cigarette.

Stuart What?

Marcus A cigarette!

Stuart You haven't smoked for years.

Marcus I've just started again!

Stuart gives Marcus a cigarette and lights it

(*Into the phone*) Paul. It's Marcus. ... It *is* important! I need to see you. ... *Now...* well, can't you re-schedule or something?... Well, when then?... No, that will be too late! It has to be tomorrow! ... No, it has to be *before* five!... (*He looks at Stuart*) I can't explain now ... but ... all right, just a minute... (*To Stuart*) Stu, do you mind? It's — it's personal.

Stuart (*heading towards the door, flustered*) No, no, of course not. I'll — I'll — I'll just get a coffee. I'll be — er — I'll just be getting a coffee if you ... if you need me...

Stuart exits

Marcus (*into the phone*) Sorry, there was someone here. ... (*He gets more agitated*) The problem? I'll tell you what the problem is! You know I phoned you last week and told you that the "gift" was disappearing, that it was regressing and that I was going to be all right? ... Well it *isn't* disappearing, it *isn't* regressing and I am *not* going to be all right! ... I *mean* that I can still see into the future as much as I could before, probably further if it's still growing, but ... What? ... No, I just *thought* it was regressing, but ... Paul, just let me tell you! ... I thought it was regressing because it was decreasing at the rate of one day per day. A week ago I could see a full week ahead — up until tomorrow. The next day I could only see six days ahead — up until tomorrow! The day after I could only see five days ahead — up until tomorrow! *Up until tomorrow!* Don't you see?... Christ, Paul, it's *obvious!* I'm still able to see into the future, I just can't see past tomorrow. .... *Yes!* ... And it's not *any time* tomorrow — it's *five o'clock* tomorrow! Five o'clock! To the second! ... I *know* because the nearer I get to it, the clearer it becomes. Paul, I can't see past five o'clock tomorrow because there's *nothing there!* There's nothing there, Paul! Nothing! . . . (*He gets tearful*) What the hell am I going to do?... I don't know what ... (*More realization. He slowly stands, dropping the phone on to the desk. He stares outward in disbelief; softly*) Oh my God ...

The Lights swiftly fade to a single tight spot on Marcus, as he is dragged back to the present

I can *see* it — in the distance — it's like a line — a distinct line — there was never a line before — I can't — I can't see past it...

The Doctor's recorded voice is heard

Doctor's voice Marcus ...
Marcus I can't see past it ... There's nothing there — no future — just — blackness ...
Doctor's voice Marcus ...
Marcus I can see it clearer now — oh, God ... (*He begins to weep into his hands*)

A single light comes up on the Doctor, who also looks outward

Doctor Marcus, can you hear me?

Marcus It's getting closer …
Doctor Marcus …
Marcus Closer …
Doctor You've got to listen to me … Can you hear me, Marcus?
   Marcus — look at me, Marcus … (*Firmly*) Look at me!

Marcus slowly looks up and outward

   Good. I want you to listen to me now…
Marcus What time is it?
Doctor Marcus, listen to me ——
Marcus The time!
Doctor It's two minutes to five. Marcus, you've got to ——
Marcus Two minutes … I'm going to be dead in two minutes …
Doctor Marcus, you're not going to die …
Marcus You kept me talking …
Doctor I promise you, you're not going to die …
Marcus Please …
Doctor It's not real, Marcus …
Marcus (*more tearful*) Help me, Paul, help me …
Doctor I will help you, if you'll let me …
Marcus Please …
Doctor Will you let me help you, Marcus?
Marcus Hurry, the line, it's getting closer …
Doctor It's not real, Marcus, it's a delusion …
Marcus Please help me …
Doctor You've had them before …
Marcus The line …
Doctor It's a symptom of psychosis …
Marcus Help me — it's getting closer …
Doctor Just focus on my voice, Marcus …
Marcus Closer …
Doctor It's not there — it's a psychosis…
Marcus No …
Doctor You've been suffering from it for two years…
Marcus No — please, no …
Doctor You've been coming here for two years — do you
   remember?

Marcus Please …
Doctor Ever since the accident …
Marcus No …
Doctor Remember the accident …
Marcus No …
Doctor You've *got* to remember, Marcus…
Marcus Please, it's nearly here — I can see it…
Doctor You've got to listen to me…
Marcus I can see it — the line — it's nearly here
Doctor She's dead, Marcus …
Marcus Please …
Doctor Clare is dead, Marcus …
Marcus No …
Doctor She died two years ago …
Marcus No …
Doctor It was a skiing accident …
Marcus No …
Doctor She was going too fast …
Marcus Please …
Doctor She lost control …
Marcus Please …
Doctor Went over the edge …
Marcus No …
Doctor Died instantly … you've got to accept it, Marcus …
Marcus No …
Doctor It's because you wouldn't accept it that you became ill …
Marcus No …
Doctor You lost everything two years ago …
Marcus Please …
Doctor You've been reliving those last two weeks over and over
  again …
Marcus No …
Doctor Hoping to change them …
Marcus No …
Doctor Hoping to change the future …
Marcus Please …
Doctor That's why you imagined you could see into the future …
Marcus No …

Doctor It is a delusion brought on by your *fear* of the future ...
Marcus No, please ...
Doctor The future without your father ...
Marcus Oh God ...
Doctor Without your work ...
Marcus Oh God ...
Doctor Without Clare ...
Marcus *Oh no!*... It's... it's not a line! It's—it's an edge—an edge
— oh my God...

*A note of panic enters the Doctor's voice. The rhythm of the now
overlapping dialogue intensifies*

Doctor Marcus, do exactly as I say...
Marcus It's coming towards me!
Doctor Focus on *me*...
Marcus Oh shit!
Doctor Marcus, focus on my voice ...
Marcus There's nothing beyond it!
Doctor Focus on *me*...
Marcus Darkness!
Doctor Please, Marcus ...
Marcus Getting nearer ...
Doctor Don't look at it ...
Marcus Nearer!
Doctor Don't look at it, Marcus!
Marcus Oh shit!
Doctor Look away!
Marcus I can hear something!
Doctor Look away from it!
Marcus It's getting louder!
Doctor Marcus!
Marcus It's... it's the wind!
Doctor Marcus, listen to me!
Marcus (*covering his ears*) So loud!
Doctor Marcus!
Marcus There it is!

Doctor No, Marcus!
Marcus It's right in front of me!
Doctor Keep away from it!
Marcus Christ!
Doctor Turn around, Marcus!
Marcus I can see over the edge!
Doctor Turn around!
Marcus It's at my feet!
Doctor Step back!
Marcus I can feel it under my feet!
Doctor Step back!
Marcus I'm slipping!
Doctor Hold on!
Marcus It's pulling me down!
Doctor Hold on, Marcus!
Marcus I'm losing my grip!
Doctor Hold on!
Marcus I can't!
Doctor Hold on!
Marcus I can't!
Doctor Marcus!
Marcus (*screaming*) *Nnnnooooo!* (*The scream is suddenly cut
    short*)

*Simultaneously, the Light on the Doctor snaps off. Marcus stares
open-mouthed and unblinking into space. A pause*

*We hear the Doctor's recorded voice, normal strength at first, then
slowly drifting off into the distance until it disappears*

Doctor's voice Marcus! Marcus! Marcus! (*etc.*)

A long pause

The Light very slowly fades out on Marcus

FURNITURE AND PROPERTY LIST

On stage: STOCKBROKER'S OFFICE
Two desks. *On them*: computers (operational), telephones,
    message pads, pens, other office equipment
Two chairs
By **Stuart'***s desk*: briefcase
Stationery cupboard. *In it*: light bulb
Coathooks or hatstand

PSYCHIATRIST'S OFFICE
Desk. *On it*: case file for **Doctor**, notepad, pen, ashtray
Two chairs

Off stage: Cup of coffee (**Stuart**)

Personal: **Marcus**: cigarettes, lighter, watch (worn throughout)
Stuart: cigarettes, lighter, watch (worn throughout)
Doctor: watch (worn throughout)

LIGHTING PLOT

Practical fittings required: overhead light fitting in stockbroker's office

Composite set: two interiors

To open: Darkness

Cue 1	When ready *Bring up lights on psychiatrist's office*	(Page 1)
Cue 2	**Marcus**: "Yes, out of synch." *Cross-fade lights from psychiatrist's office to stockbroker's office*	(Page 3)
Cue 3	Popping sound *Black-out*	(Page 6)
Cue 4	**Stuart**: "Another coincidence, I suppose." *Snap on stockbroker's office lights*	(Page 7)
Cue 5	**Marcus** hangs up *Cross-fade office lighting to two tight spots on **Marcus** and the **Doctor***	(Page 8)
Cue 6	**Marcus**: "That's when I came to see you." *Fade light slowly on **Doctor***	(Page 9)
Cue 7	**Marcus**: " ... a red coat, for some reason —— " *Slowly cross- fade light on **Marcus** to light on **Doctor***	(Page 9)
Cue 8	**Doctor**: " ... without knowing how we know it." *Bring up full lights on psychiatrist's office*	(Page 9)

Cue 9   **Marcus/ Doctor**: "PENGUIN!"   (Page 11)
             Black-out

Cue 10   **Stuart**'s phone rings   (Page 11)
             Bring up lights on stockbroker's office

Cue 11   **Stuart** tries to find information on his computer   (Page 11)
             Bring up lights on psychiatrist's office

Cue 12   **Doctor**: " ... your father's funeral ... "   (Page 13)
             Fade lights on psychiatrist's office

Cue 13   **Stuart**: "We've been rumbled."   (Page 16)
             Cross-fade lights from stockbroker's office
                to single spot on **Doctor**

Cue 14   **Doctor**: " ... another contributory factor."   (Page 16)
             Bring up lights on psychiatrist's office

Cue 15   **Marcus**: "He was on the phone when I got there ..."(Page 17)
             Cross-fade lights from psychiatrist's office
                to stockbroker's office

Cue 16   **Marcus**: "Oh my God ... "   (Page 21)
             Cross-fade office lights to single tight spot
                on **Marcus**

Cue 17   **Marcus** weeps into his hands   (Page 21)
             Bring up single light on **Doctor**

Cue 18   **Marcus**'s scream is suddenly cut short   (Page 25)
             Snap off light on **Doctor**

Cue 19   **Doctor**: "Marcus! Marcus! Marcus!"   (Page 25)
             Fade light on **Marcus** — *very slowly*

EFFECTS PLOT